FIRESIDE SERIES

Ramtha

Jesus
The Christ
The Life of a Master

JESUS THE CHRIST — THE LIFE OF A MASTER

ISBN # 1-57873-059-7

JZK Publishing
A Division of JZK, Inc.

Ramtha's School of Enlightenment
P.O. Box 1210
Yelm, Washington 98597
360.458.5201
800.347.0439
www.ramtha.com
www.jzkpublishing.com

These series of teachings are designed for all the students of the Great Work who love the teachings of the Ram.

It is suggested that you create an ideal learning environment for study and contemplation.

Light your fireplace and get cozy. Prepare yourself. Open your mind to learn and be genius.

FOREWORD

The Fireside Series is an ongoing library of the hottest topics of interest taught by Ramtha. These series of teachings are designed for all the students of the Great Work who love the teachings of the Ram. This collection is also intended as a continuing learning tool for the students of Ramtha's School of Enlightenment and for everyone interested and familiar with Ramtha's teachings. In the last three decades Ramtha has continuously and methodically deepened and expanded his exposition of the nature of reality and its practical application through various disciplines. It is assumed by the publisher that the reader has attended a Beginning Retreat or workshop through Ramtha's School of Enlightenment or is at least familiar with Ramtha's instruction to his beginning class of students. This introductory information is found in *Ramtha: A Beginner's Guide to Creating Reality*, Third Ed. (Yelm: JZK Publishing, a division of JZK, Inc., 2004).

We have included in the Fireside Series a glossary of some of the basic concepts used by Ramtha so the reader can become familiarized with these teachings. We have also included a brief introduction of Ramtha by JZ Knight that describes how all this began for those who are unfamiliar with the story. Enjoy your learning and contemplation.

CONTENTS

THE PATH OF A CHRIST:
RISKING EVERYTHING FOR THE SAKE OF TRUTH

The first Sunday that was ever celebrated in the Great Hall and when this school was finally cemented to be here was Easter Sunday.[1] The teaching was about the resurrection of Christ, a life well-lived, a man who realized God and put it all on the line. "Look, you may crucify my body but that doesn't change my truth, because what you destroy today I will re-create within moments." That puts it on the line, doesn't it?

What is so beautiful about Yeshua ben Joseph is that even in myth he was exalted as being this great, powerful, wise, loving teacher. His message, thought to be original at that time, is an original message that did belong to him: "The kingdom of heaven is within and I am both the son of man and the son of God. As the son of man I am fragile, I am tempted, I am afraid, I am insecure, but as the son of God I belong to the ages. And there is no-thing that you can do to me that my Father in heaven has not approved."

We love that. It makes us weep inside. And we get closer to it because we think that if we worship it, somehow that greatness and that divine flawless life will rub off on us. That is why we weep when we hear the story of Jesus. He was a great man who was the legal heir to the throne of Judea. He came from a royal house, and it was his job to transmute being the son of man into the son of God. It was his job to do that, but he had a passion for it. That Easter Sunday that we were here was a blustery day and I said to all of you, so what is the mystique of Christ? Christ means the Christos, to know. What that says is that he knew something. He knew it and he lived it.

1 Easter Sunday, March 26, 1989. The Great Hall is the main auditorium where classes are held at Ramtha's School of Enlightenment in Yelm, Washington.

Many people can know things philosophically, theoretically, but they don't live them. They somehow separate themselves from their knowingness. They live in sort of a psychosis, an area of their mind to which they know but never live the knowingness because living is somehow separate from this knowingness. You will hear people say, and I have heard you say, "Inside of me I know better. I know what the truth is but I don't live it." Why? Is there some element to you that says that truth already is truth if it is realized and does not beg us to live by our own realization? What an interesting concept, masters. Why do you know so much and live it so little?

Is then the action part of your life what is meaningful? I will tell you, it is your image and your body that are meaningful to you, and then somehow over here in this little box you have got the great knowingness sitting that you sort of worship but never have to become. The reason that you love Christ is because Christ put it on the line. A man put it on the line and he was willing then to live his truth so that the idea of being the son of man became wretched to him because he realized that sons and daughters of men and women live life but the sons and daughters of God are inhibited from it.

We love him because he was a brave man. We idolize him because he does what we couldn't do, what we would hope we could do but most people could never do because their greatest fear is death. The greatest fear is death, and that can be the death of an image, the death of a relationship, the death of a family, the loss of economic support. Death is a fearful thing: the loss of youth, the loss of beauty, the loss of limbs. And if you take all of those and find what is the common denominator, it is loss, it is death.

So how much greater could Christ have been than you? He was an entity that put it all on the line, everything. When someone says to you, "I will give you your life if you recant," you think about it. All I have to do is say I am sorry, all I have to do is plead as if I am ignorant, and if I do that then my life will be salvaged. But a great mind such as a Christ knows that once we prostitute truth for the subtleties of life, we are already dead.

The first message when I came here was that you are God and that the Christ is your opportunity. But you conjure up some sort of awful dread. It could be as near as mastering this important part of your life, your image, your body, that a Christ could be as near as incorporating that beautiful truth into a living light. It could be that close. How close is that? Well, it could be as close as to say what have I got to lose? Maybe I will gain everything. What have I got to lose by changing? What have I got to lose to give up my superficial ignorance? Maybe what I gain is knowledge and freedom. But then your mind goes to work and says, yes, but if you give that up, here are the consequences. Now we know why Christs were so rare, because they gave it all up. When you are willing to die for what you know, that is the moment you are truly the most alive.

This teaching that I did this Easter Sunday really kicked this school off in these quarters. It was a beautiful, unforgettable morning. It was haunting. The object of the teaching was to say that every one of you need not ever worship a mental idea or indeed a mental dream again. The Christ is not to be worshiped as an idol but as an ideal to be loved and admired and inspired by.

The greatest being that lives within you is the one that is the son or the daughter of the living God. Who is the living God? Your Holy Spirit. It is really the fundamental that holds your whole reality together. But we have a problem in mastery, we do, and the problem is that you think you are going to lose when you change, so now you are going to miss life. Maybe you have been missing it all along. So what do you say about that? Over here is your life, your friends, your enemies, your lovers, your husbands, wives, your children, your beliefs, your knowledge, your ignorance, your prejudices, your limitations, your accomplishments. And then right here is the message of God, the great life, the worthy life. How do we then merge the two together? Rarely are they ever merged because people want to worship philosophically, ideally, a lofty thing but they never want to live it. Why? And I am going to ask you that question: Why would you want to?

Yeshua ben Joseph had a wife. He knew what it was to make love to a woman and he knew what it was to have children. Did that cease his message? His message was enriched. Don't you think he understood people? Yes. So what did he do that was different than you? What are we talking about here? This is what he did. The greatest teaching that was ever taught was the teaching on the mount.[2] He said to his people who wanted to know how to find the kingdom of heaven, love your neighbor as yourself. We could go on and explain that a little bit further in this twenty-first century of open sexual relationships. We could also say love yourself as you labor to love your partner. I loved that message, and he wasn't the first to say it. Anyone who was a master already knew that. And there were many masters before Yeshua ben Joseph, great ones, and there were many after him. It becomes not a singular knowingness but an all-knowingness.

Who suffers in life? I will tell you who suffers in life. Our Spirit suffers to the preference of our bodies. Let me explain that further. What is the Spirit? The Spirit is the invisible voice. It is the invisible knowingness. It is our greatness undeveloped.

A master does the opposite of what you do. You work to develop your social life. You work to develop your bodies. You work to develop your relationship, your beauty, your rapport. Why, you even work and labor to develop your victimization. You do. You know it is the truth. A master does the opposite. A master's journey is not about developing the psychosis of the physical life. The master's

---

2 Gospel according to Matthew 5:1-7:29, The Sermon on the Mount.

journey is to develop the spiritual life. What is the spiritual life? The spiritual life is to live a life flawlessly, based upon that which is termed the highest concepts of what we are. And what we are transcends genders, all genders. Literally we are talking about a life that is really dedicated to taking this knowingness and then making that life. That is what a master is. To a master there are not two different aspects to self, the spiritual, and then the physical image. A master takes and develops the spiritual in front of the body.

People who are body/mind consciousness literally starve to death their spiritual life because too many times the way they get partners, sexual partners, the way that they get to become victims is based upon a body/mass subjugation. Now that is the physical. It works in all realms. A spiritual being, a master, goes after that which they know.

The difference between you and Yeshua ben Joseph is that Yeshua ben Joseph knew that he was born to be God and so his life was dedicated to being the son of God, even though he was born of a man. And when he was weak he acknowledged, "It is my humanity. It is not the Father within me. The Father within me is the all-wise, knowing intelligence."

That Easter Sunday morning, in this Great Hall and under that tree in stormy weather, we truly celebrated Jesus' life and all masters' lives who chose to live the path of the master. We celebrated his resurrection, celebrated that he truly lived as the son of God and thereby rejoiced. That is why he could put it on the line. He was a being that was gifted with the royal blood. He was an entity that had everything going for him, and he could certainly seduce with that kind of power. But people who misuse that sort of power always end up in the most wretched lives. It works in the moment but it will catch up with them.

Jesus was an entity who put aside the woman that he loved, his children, the throne, and had a message. The message was, "In order for me to be the king of the Jews, I must first be the son of God and so I must live my life in that refrain and not that I am the son of my mother and my father. Everyone can be the sons and daughters of their parents, but very few ever finally decide to say I am the royal blood of my Holy Spirit and this is the life that I must live."

Love Who You Are First

What does this have to do with relationships? Well, there are a lot of women and men in this audience that need to understand something, that to love another person means the unequivocal love of yourself. Loving yourself isn't about buffing your fingernails and it is not about the hairdo that you have. It is not about the muscles you have or the breasts that you have or how many times you starve yourself so you can be thin. You do that and you know that you do that. That is not about loving yourself. Loving yourself is living to your highest moral and spiritual aptitude. That is loving yourself, and to love another person is only equal to what you feel about yourself spiritually.

Anyone can be a body. We can take everyone in this audience, young and old alike, and give yourself to me for ninety days. If you want to make a body, I know how to make a body. Not only are you going to be buff, you are going to be analogical and you can do anything. I know how to use muscles. That is not what I am here for. I am not here for that, and you should be glad.

Now, masters, let me get back to this subject matter because it is important. If we spent as much time developing our great moral mind, if we spent as much time developing our spiritual self — not our carnal self; carnal selves come easy; spiritual selves don't because they are undeveloped — then we can love someone. Then that someone doesn't have to be a someone that needs us so much in order for their life to continue. We can love someone and dedicate our precious temple, which the body is then. If God is made manifest, then the body becomes the holy temple. Then we can share the temple and ritual, with someone that we love, clean and virtuous and honorably. That is all right. It is beautiful. But if we are scoundrels, if we suffer from the psychosis of our image, we will never be faithful to anyone. Moreover, we will never be honest with anyone because we have never been that to ourselves. If we had, we wouldn't be in a dishonest relationship.

If we had indeed revered ourselves and honored ourselves, if we understood that our semen — for men, because I was a man — was alive, men of virtue don't spill their seed unless it is in the name of love and sharing, and that could only be equal to who we are. We can love another because of the love we have for ourself. "I give you the gift of my seed. I have not spilt it through masturbation daily because I am in a habit of doing that. I have honored myself and treasured myself and loved myself, and when I give myself to you, it is truly a gift." That is a moral person.

Are there such people? Yes. Have there been such people? Yes, great people, great men and women. What are Christs? They know that the semen is alive and they know that it is energy, and if they do not spill it needlessly they can use the energy right into their brain to focus on that which is termed perfecting the moral life.

Christ also said forgive your debtors that in essence you may be forgiven. Debts always mean a past. Any master who wants to be a master does not have a debt because that is the past and it is not the present. When we forgive those who owe us, then we are freed up to live in the present, and that is more precious. To the person we may forgive, they may think we are a fool. They may celebrate our kind heart, but they have just been released from their honor.

So what is a true master? One who is so present, cannot occupy the space of the past, and forgives those who owe them money. Now you begin to see why the lofty ideal up here has no commonplace practicality in life. A Christ doesn't go after the practicality in life but to make known the spiritual image of God.

It is true, there are elder people in this school who have heard these words many times but you have never been as evolved as you are this moment. Perhaps you begin to understand what I am telling you, that in the divine present, in the moment, this box that we see out of our frontal lobe, we want to clean it up. We do not want that only this much of our box is all that we have available for manifesting greatness while every day we have to keep renewing our past, our debts, our loves, our angers, our hatreds, our selfishness, our image, that it takes so much of the moment up. No wonder we are spiritually starved. The mind is starved. It takes a mindless person to keep it going. You know why? Because the mind is the phenomenon. The mind is the extraordinary. The mind is the emulous creature that creates reality.

It doesn't take a brilliant person to keep laying on every moment the past, anger, resentment, failure, success, sickness, enemies. It just takes a habit. It just takes a life. It just takes hormones.

Becoming Clear As Little Children

Now this is the truth, and I will tell you why it is the truth. I have really arrogant, body-physical people in this school. They think they know it all. But I have got children that would put them to shame. They are so clean and so innocent. They have no sexuality. They have no image to grind. They are just children.

You know why? Because little children already are the purest Spirit they will ever be when they are little children. They don't have testosterone. They do not have female hormones. They do not have images. They don't have breasts and penises and they don't have muscles. They don't have faces and hair and all of that other stuff that gets in the way. They are just purely themselves, without an image. How do you explain that? How would Christ explain it? He would say, "Don't keep them away. Don't you know that the kingdom of heaven is like these little children? The very message that I have to offer to you is like them, and the way that you enter the kingdom of heaven is to be like one of them."

What is he saying? They are innocent. They don't have enemies. They don't have loves. They have dreams. They don't have vaginas and penises and muscles and faces and hairdos and wealth. They don't have diseases. They are clean. Well, all of you have been clean. What is he saying? "You have to be like one of these children to know what I know." It is such a beautiful teaching.

I love my children because they have demonstrated that the window of the divine moment can manifest anything you want — anything. Then what is the secret? To be that clear, that clean, that innocent. I don't care if you are a hundred and eighty years old and you have eight hundred children, can you still be innocent? Yes. What does innocence mean? When the moment is not contaminated by the past or the image.

THE BIRTH OF A CHRIST

I want you to know something — actually, I want you to know everything — that no one except the great masters of antiquity and those who were public about the teachings ever said that you too are a Christ and that you are God. That is what was so outrageous. That was blasphemy. It is blasphemy in the West. It is blasphemy in the East. It is blasphemy in the North. And if you are truly going to conquer your image, it is real blasphemy in the South. I like it. Might as well be an original. The same as Yeshua ben Joseph, I have a message and I am going to deliver the message. The people who try to destroy it are destroying it because the message undermines the lifestyle that they have grown accustomed to living, and the message is you are God. Don't you think it is time you acted like one?

What kind of impact does it have on your life? Well, to certain masters of antiquity it cost them their life. Again think about the children who go and do Fieldwork℠ or do The Tank® or do archery, sending-and-receiving, how magnificent they are. The children that are on the cusp of innocence and puberty, what did they give up? When they go to the field, they give up a day of playing. They give up a day of being irresponsible. It is hard for you to think that way, but they do sacrifice in order to do what they do. What is so beautiful about them is that they are totally present, and they know that when Fieldwork℠ is over they will get to go play again. But in the meantime a God is being coaxed out of the body, and that is what I am here to do.

Arrogant people in this school will never understand the glory of Yeshua ben Joseph because they think that you are not really living unless you are copulating, unless you are drinking, unless you are in the image, unless you are in style, unless you are in fashion, unless you are young and beautiful. Women in this audience, many of you still think that your life isn't any kind of life unless you are beautiful, sexual, and can hold a man by those aspects. You have never given another thought about what will happen when all of that wanes. You don't give a thought about that. To the disagreeable amongst you, the image says, "But if I live my life for these teachings, if I go out every day and I do Fieldwork[SM], if I create my day every day, if I live according to the Sermon on the Mount, if I live that way I would be missing a lot of life." No, you wouldn't. The trap is you think you are because your body's hormones say you are missing some life. But in the meantime what really happens is you begin to elongate life and a lot of biological, wonderful things start to happen to you.

I tell you the most sublime and beautiful of men is a man who walks in grace, who is impeccable to his spiritual self, who loves himself not for the reflection in the mirror but for what comes out of his eyes, what is spoken from his lips, what he feels in the tears that he sheds. That is a beautiful man, a man who is not ashamed to accept back one hundred years everything that he has said, a man who is honest, a man who is not opportunistic, a man who uses his mind in the most brilliant of ways and understands that the most satisfying thing at the end of the day is not a roll in the hay but how much were you able to influence your own life from a loftier perspective.

A great and beautiful woman is not a woman judged upon her face, her figure, like so many of you are involved in. That is not life. The natural biology of your life has given you a pleasant time in life to where you are the most beautiful and blushed with the opportunity to bear children. You have the figure, you have the breasts, you have the uterus, you have the face. That is only for a moment. That is only for the sake of capturing and copulating. True beauty is not to do with one's body. It is the originality of the Spirit, the dancing eyes, and the mind that is quick, a

Spirit that knows and understands challenges in life, that does not depend upon other people, does not depend upon another man, and does not spend her life trapping a man. A spiritual Christ that is female is truly an awesome thing to behold, and it is admirable and rarer than two moons in the sky.

This is an entity self-contained within their own power who falls in love with themselves. When you love yourself you perfect the thoughts, you perfect the actions, you perfect the dreams, that suddenly the center of your nucleus is not someone else but yourself. The center of joy is not someone else but yourself, doing those things that bring to you a happiness and a sense of glee at night, that what you did was greater than your body, your genetics, and your gender. At night you realize the great things that you lived for that day, that transcended the relationships in your life, made you wiser, more beautiful, and more spiritual.

What are we to expect when we go home? A change in values, a richer, truer, more beautiful self that if the whole world isn't happy about, you can put it on the line and even die for it because it brings you joy. So what do you do with all of this training? Have you really lived, or are you just hurrying up trying to do that? I tell you, life is a gift. It is beautiful. But I also tell you that a person who lives in the valley, who only looks at the mountains and wonders about them but is only concerned with valley consciousness, is the same as if you lived on top of the mountain and saw it all. There is much more to life.

When you develop the body, oftentimes you starve the mind. You starve the mind for the sake of bodies, your chemical reactions, because you are a bag of chemicals, you know. You starve that for the fulfillment and you think that is living. Did it ever occur to you that maybe living is a higher order, a mind that is so sharp and so powerful it can manifest anything? Does that exclude the body? No, the body becomes the perfect temple of a great and masterful leader.

Does this mean you will never have sexual relationships again? No, but it means that they will be more cherished, more real, more in the moment, and not artificial. Does it mean that you are going to miss out on business opportunities? No, it just will make you wiser, more clever, and more knowing. You will be light-years ahead of the game. Does it mean indeed that you have missed out on seeing the world? Once you have seen the world in only a microcosm of here and there, you will realize how ignorant the world really is.

Purpose of the Schools of Ancient Wisdom: God Realized in a Human Being

So, my beautiful people, Easter Sunday morning I also said to everyone, you are a Christ, one who knows, God/man and God/woman realized. I also said it takes a moment to know that but it takes the rest of your life to live it. And therein lies the reason for the Ancient School of Wisdom, because no one knows how to teach it. I will tell you why, because everyone teaches it with deep consideration for the body and they don't really understand any of the spiritual aspects at all. Spiritual to them is sort of a nebulous thing, but I tell you that the Spirit is what is hidden and suppressed behind our bodies. It is the higher thinking order. It is the higher knowing order. And as you have all learned now, the more you know, the greater your kingdoms.[3]

Spirit is not about being good or bad. It is about being God, which is neither. The body is about being good and bad. The image is about being good and bad. The Spirit is not about being any of those things, and God is just the enforcer of your wishes.

---

3 See *Buddha's Neuronet for Levitation*. Fireside Series, Vol. 2, No. 4, revised edition. (Yelm: JZK Publishing, a division of JZK, Inc., 2006).

The day that we paid tribute to the day that Yeshua ben Joseph rose from the dead and conquered death is because he was willing to put it all on the line. Let us look at that in respect to what you have learned. If consciousness and energy creates everything, then he wouldn't have been afraid for his life because consciously he knew that he would never die and indeed that he has lived before and will live again. That is putting it on the line. So where did he put his odds? He put his odds on his Spirit. He said, "I am with my Holy Spirit. You can do anything to my body but you will never destroy me." And he was right. On the other hand, a person that is wholly their body will always say, "If you torture me, I will do anything you want because I can't stand pain and I am filled with fear." And therein lies the basis of many relationships. So what kind of relationship are you having? If you are having the latter, you are having an empty, nonprogressive relationship and you are the culprit.

So why don't you do the work, because you think you already know it? If you really knew it, you could do as good as my children do. But you don't know it, you see. It is about being innocent in the moment and not having people, places, things, times, and events, just the desire.

Why wouldn't you want to participate? It is about learning the secret that children know and what you used to know, that everything was possible and that dreams are bigger than life. If that is so, the children are right because anything that is bigger than life must be life itself.

What is it to work up to that point that when you think of Yeshua ben Joseph, you do get tears in your eyes and you think of all the great people who seemingly didn't live the fun-frolicking life for something much more poignant. And where are they today? You wonder, don't you? You wonder where they went. Maybe they really knew what life was about. Maybe you are just guessing at it. Maybe you are being led around by your body instead of your Spirit.

Children have that sweet innocence that every master has to become again. When masters leave no footprints, it really means they are childlike. It means that they go to work on something. They don't think about anyone, any time, any past, any event, anything except their desire. That is pure innocence and that is pure clarity. If you will note, they are not highly intellectual so that means then that the gift of innocence will be taught out of them and replaced with the intellectual, emotional body. Is that an experience? Yes.

So what do they have to do with Christ? He said very plainly, "Why are you pushing them away? This is like the kingdom of heaven, and the only way you get into the kingdom of heaven, the great life, is when you can become one of them." What does that mean? It means they are just children. They don't have sexual relationships going on. They don't have diseases they have created. They don't have victimizations. They don't have suffering. And they don't know they are out of style until someone tells them. It is just being children. That is beautiful.

That is so rare, but that is what it takes to be a God, a Christ, who can put it all on the line and say, "I know you don't believe me. I know you don't believe anything I have said. I know that all of the things I have said have challenged your box, challenged your bodies, challenged your beliefs. I know you don't believe me and you are going to crucify me because I am a challenge. I make you restless. I trouble you. You can't get me off your mind because what I am saying is really in defense of your Spirit and not your body/mind consciousness. I know you don't like me. I know you severely don't like me. You don't like me so much that you would like to kill me, destroy me, get rid of me. I know all of that, but I am saying the message anyway. I know my life is in danger and the only way you are going to silence me is to kill me. But I will tell you this. What I have said, I have said in the witness of my Holy Spirit and my God. And I have taught you what no one would teach you. One day you are going to hit the light and you are going to know the truth and you are going to wish like hell that you had listened." That is what he said to them. And he said, "You can destroy my body, but I will resurrect it in the twinkling of an eye. Then you will have an enemy forever and ever and ever. And who is your enemy? Your guilt, your lack, your ignorance, and your own prejudice."

Now that message was appropriate that sweet Sunday morning — stormy morning in the West, the shores of Lemuria — because that really was the christening of the Great Hall and this property for a school that would finally teach a splendid few to walk the Spirit and not the body, to feel so confident, and to know so richly of what you speak that no one can ever take it away from you, it is that clean and that pure, and to love yourself so enormously that no matter what anyone does to your body, you will not strike back at them because you know that whatever they do, they have committed the great sin and you can repair it at any moment and that you will live on and on and on. What is a limited lifetime in the breath of all eternity?

The Moral Code of a Master

The school is based on you are God and God becomes a Christ in men and women. The school was to purify that in all of its disciplines, its obvious unobvious teachings, its understanding. "I can't go back to my mother's womb to be born again, and the only way I am going to be born again is if I die. I don't wish to die now. I wish to be born again, to be awakened here and now." Well, here and now is just understanding that it is time to put into importance the spiritual rather than the physical, because if the spiritual takes center stage then you will love yourself and be able to love your lover, your mother, your father, your children, your friends. You will be able to forgive your debtors because they belong to the past. We can't have the moment of clarity if we are a landlord, if we are a creditor enslaving the poor wretchedness of our debtors, because they are wretched.

We can never have that clean moment as long as we have a debtor. And what is more important, getting the money or forgiving? It is forgiving that is more important because in that we are clean. If we don't forgive, we are always connected to them, and it is yesterday and it occupies the moment that truly that which is termed the extraordinary mind can manifest. We forgive them.

What if you are a debtor? When you have been forgiven, what has been taken from you, relaxed to you, is that your debt is abolished. But what is the next step for the debtor? The next step for the debtor, in order to abolish it from their present, honors its commitment. Now we start to find impeccable men and women — impeccable — that even if it is abolished by the one they owe, it will not be abolished in their life. You know why? Because it will be a guilt, it will be that which has been unhonorable, and we will always find ways to hate them, to undermine them, to talk about them, to crucify them. We are only doing that to cover up our own shame. They are flawless. They forgave us. What a pristine moment. We can't even handle it. We have to make them the bad guy. Now we are talking spiritual integrity.

Love your father and your mother, yes. You know why? They gave you life. They were a copulating couple. Regardless of how they ended up in life, they gave you the temple of God and you forever love them for that. Are they responsible for your life? No, they have already given it to you. It is you who are responsible for it, to love them and to honor them always. I don't care what they did to you. I don't care how they abandoned you. I don't care their neglect. I don't care their religion. I don't care their persuasions. I don't care. You honor them because they gave you life. You should never blame them for your life. They gave you the body. You are the Holy Spirit who is responsible for the body, not them. That is beautiful.

So what do you do? You forgive yourself and your stupidity. You forgive yourself. And the moment you do that you will understand your parents and you will love and honor them. To love and honor them doesn't mean you have to move back in with them to show them your affection or to call them up and borrow money. I am not talking about that. That is not love and honor. That is burden. It is just to honor them. "You gave me life." To my mother, beautiful young lass, "You gave me life. You stretched out your body and I suckled at your breast, and you gave up a lot of your beauty so that I could be. I honor you for that." And for my father, "I honor you that I inherited your name. I honor you that you gave me a part of yourself in your genetics. I honor you for the human that you have been. And no matter what you do I shall always love you, for you gave me the opportunity to be born again."

That is all there is. It is not "and they did this, and I did that, and they did this, and I did that." It is not any of that. That is how a master thinks. They honor them because if that is all there is, then you are free to clean up your moment.

To love your God with all of your might, love the Lord God of your being with all of your might and all of your life, well, who is God? It is not Jehovah and indeed it is not the pantheon of the Gods. It is that from which you sprang, that which is the entity occupying the temple. To love it with all of your might and all of your life is inclusive, to love and to honor it. To go against your Spirit is a spiritual transgression that is the pain in the soul. That is our deepest, darkest haunting. But when we love it and honor it, then we love and honor it in other people.

Everyone who knows this wants their frontal lobe clean, like a bride who prepares her wedding bed for her groom. We prepare our mind as a wedding bed for our husbandman, our God, the Holy Spirit, and we marry it. The body marries this Holy Spirit. Now we have Christ walking on the earth. Are they happy beings? Always. Would they ever enter into a relationship for the convenience of money, sexuality, looks, and convenience? Never. Would they ever have a relationship based on any of these things? Never, ever. Would they ever blame anyone? Never. And most things that go wrong are not that person's error but their own shortsightedness. That is a master speaking.

If a teacher two thousand years ago who was the rightful heir to a royal throne was required by his heritage, his creed, and his law to be not only a king but a righteous teacher of the people, then that was a master who had learned mastership and could lead and teach those people the righteous path without prejudice and bias, no matter what it took.

Here at school we have then the same situation occurring. I don't care what it takes, as long as you can drop all the dross in your life and come back to clarity. My job here is to take you on the same journey and not a journey that only a few have ever made, but it is possible for every one of you: every man, woman, and child, no matter your color, no matter your creed, no matter your origin, no matter how beautiful, how ugly. That is why I came back here, and the school was commenced upon Easter Sunday in the resurrection of the Christ who said, "This is the law. This is the way that it is. And I am willing to lay down my life though no other will, though those who are closest to me will flee from me and deny me. The people that I trusted will deny me and I am left naked. It is still the truth. You may not like it and you have the law to take my life, but I have the law to resurrect it and I will."

FEAR OF DEATH AND
THE ART OF ASCENSION

Yeshua ben Joseph, for all that he knew, did not make one of his disciples or apostles a master. They were philosophers even though he said to them, "Everything I have done, you can do a lot better. Just do it."[4] They never did do it. Not one of Yeshua ben Joseph's followers ever became a master.

People are peculiar animals. They are intrinsically devoted to their sexuality. They are intrinsically devoted to their emotions. They are intrinsically devoted to their domain. And to unroot them has nearly been impossible for every great voice that cried out in the wilderness for eons. All the great artistic works, the literary works, all the great poets and great prophets endeavored to inspire, to awaken, and to give this message to people who only found it religious or artful, to put it in its own little box, nice and tidy, and never went any further with it, never were inspired by it.

How many people in your life have ever told you you are a God and how many people in your life ever told you you were great just on your own? The reason you are here is because I have told you things that no other entity in the whole world has ever told you, that no other culture ever respects. Everyone has got bits and pieces but no one has everything. The people that have everything don't live here anymore. They moved on. People that live here still don't know.

Who has ever told you that you were really great and that you could do anything and that you were greater than your body, greater than your image, greater than

---

4 Gospel according to John 14:12.

your lethargicness, that you are really God? I have to ask you, maybe you don't want to hear that. Maybe you are one of those people who destroys the good message because the good message means you have to change. Maybe you are one of those destroyers. How far are you from that Christ who put his life on the line? They killed this man.

You know why I love my injured people? Because they went after it. They created the injuries, yes, but they lived through them. They went after it and didn't have any fear. I got run through by a sword, and I was pretty savvy in my lifetime — the son of God was killed by crazy people — but we went after it.

Remember I told you the story about the great masters you wouldn't even recognize? You wouldn't look at them because they are not beautiful. They have got half their ears chewed off and they have got scars down their neck, on the arm, a finger missing. Well, how could that be a master? All of those are lessons. I kept my scar till the day that I left here. I loved it. It changed my life. It brought me down from my haughty existence to my mortality. When I really realized I did bleed is the day I became a little concerned and I decided to change it. So you wouldn't recognize us. Even if you wanted to see a master, you think they are running around with those UFOs above your heads and all have blond hair down to the ground and these big, bulky, not-useful wings. The human shoulder blades cannot flex fast enough to lift you off of the ground. And besides that, even if you had them how would that change your fashion? Well, that is something else to consider.

How far are you then from the greatness that you cry about but have been too weak to ever become? This school isn't about dying. It is about becoming greater than what you ever thought you could be. If Christ then is that daring original that makes us cry, how many opportunities are we given to be that original, to put it all on the line? Every day in this school is about that. Every discipline is about that. I don't want any of you to die. I want you to live. You are the ones who insist on dying. You are the ones who insist upon thinking limited. You are the ones who insist upon your fears, not me. I am outrageous. I want you to be so awesome that at the end of the day you are in a mood of ecstasy because you are both crying and screaming and dancing all at the same time because you overcame something that was your nemesis. So beautiful.

One man against Rome, one man against the powers in Jerusalem, one man and twelve very fearful followers, what a righteous entity. You have to love this entity. You have to love him. He was outrageous and fearless. He was outrageous and wonderful because he loved all people, not just Jews. He loved all people. What an outrageous entity. It was enough to live his life for it.

Why can't you do that? Why can't you live for greatness? That is outrageous. It is beautiful, not a hypocrite and not a diplomat, not one that sat on the middle of the fence. I tell you there is nothing that tires me more than these cosmic talkers amongst you or these intellectuals amongst you that like to spin mind labyrinths, that are so full of it. They can't even do the work. Let's live it. Can you live it? Then I will admire you.

I am talking about Easter Sunday when we remembered a being who was just loving and powerful and a true priest among his people, a true master amongst his disciples, who was outrageous, unique, and beautiful. And we love him to this day. How rare are they? How many masters can you count on one hand? Did he ever really live life? Yes. What about afterlife, the kingdom of heaven, life forever and ever and ever? That is what happens when you switch the image of your personality to the image of God, you switch a short life of seventy-five or eighty or maybe ninety years. The last part is always filled with pain and disease if you choose that over something that is immortal and great.

This school is about teaching you how to be a Christ, men and women, and how to set aside your little prejudices, walk the line and do the work, and not be afraid. To do sending-and-receiving, to learn to read another person's mind, maybe if you learn to do that you won't be such a fool. To be able to know your future is really good because then you will never be a victim to your choices. This is greatness and it is outrageous. That is why I am here, to teach you that for a little period of time.

Now I am happy to report that I have more than twelve people. There is still a lot of polishing ahead, but we are not that far away. I also want to tell you this, that if you were able to do all of this work so far, then the next stage of the work about increasing body frequency through the mind — not leaving the body but increasing body time — is as simple as finding your card in the field. It is not impossible. It is totally natural. If the mind can speed the heart rate up or slow it down, the mind can also speed body time. Now the trick is to convince the mind. How do we convince the mind? The mind is made by that which is termed the intent of the personality on the brain. When the brain can hold the intent, the design, then the mind is convinced. And the moment the mind is convinced, we have a dramatic altercation that happens between the past paradigms of reality and the present paradigms of reality. Time is measured through consciousness.

The next level will be addressing the teaching of how we raise the frequency of body time to displace the body in time and to replace it. This is the beginning of the art of ascension, not leaving the body, not leaving the house behind to let it decay but changing the time of the house, that we take it to the Plane of Bliss.

So obviously that art then, in order for that to occur, has got to be like a little child again. You tell them to do it, they just do it. When I teach you to do it, you just do it. It is not dragging in the consequences of the past laid upon the future, the relationship, the children, the no-children, the rejection, the acceptance, the pain, the suffering, the disease, the passion, the nonpassion, the abandonment, the embrace, the sexual dysfunction. So obviously you have to be good at not being any of those things, and then we can do it.

JESUS' FINAL INITIATION

Yeshua ben Joseph knew that however he saw anything is exactly how he agreed for it to be. When he saw the blind man, the blind man asked for help. He bent over, picked up some clay, and he spat in it. What he was doing with the clay and his spit was creating a new biofield of particle relationship. When he did this and put it on the blind man's eyes, in molding the clay Yeshua ben Joseph saw perfect vision. As he was molding the clay, the clay became the catalyst for perfect vision. When he put the clay on his eyes, that biofield or morphogenic field reconstructed immediately the visual nerve supply to the back of the brain and he saw instantly.

We call that a miracle-worker. How powerful is it to be like this entity, who every day of his life worked up to this level of relationship with the particle field? What did he have to do? Walking down the path he would see and choose immediately whether to agree with the landscape or change it. If he was walking and stirring up saffron dust and found delight in that, then he was agreeing with the dust and the dust never changed. How many times do you walk down the path and stir up dust and are agitated with it? That only enforces its nature.

If he walked into a group of people, is teaching them, then stops to feed them and he has only a basket of fishes and a loaf of bread and has five thousand people, what would your mind say? Let's run to the market straightaway; correct? This was a master who understood the relationship between mind and matter and all he had to do was to change his mind on what he saw. So the fish and the bread became the seed that multiplied in his mind, and as long as he saw it, the supply was endless. Now where did the supply come from? The supply came from one fish and one loaf of bread, and all he needed to do was to make them multitudinous. So what he did is he kept creating echoes of the fish and the bread, and he was taking energy that was falling apart and recoagulating it, giving them a frame of reference to coagulate into.

If you stop and think about it, someone told the rose to be a rose and someone told it how to smell and someone or something described to the rose in a mental thought deep, velvet red. Someone did that because it didn't just spring up on its own. It was created to be what it is, not only the rose but birds and water and the environment. Someone focused them into evolution. Who was that? You.

Yeshua ben Joseph was considered a master all the way up to the sixth level. His job, as difficult as it was, was to defy reality with his mind. If I am telling you today that what you think affects all life around you, then if you stop for a moment and reflect, you will see how your life has stayed static according to your image thoughts. You drive down the city, you expect to see the city, the city is there. You expect to see people begging, they are always there. You expect to see a car wreck on the side of the road because you need a little excitement, there is always one. If that is true and you have the power, imagine what an initiation it was for such a being, and beings, that every day they had to defy physical reality and overlay with a mind so powerful that they could see what was not there and make it that. Powerful.

Do you think that that is more powerful than you? No, it is you. Where is your energy? Your energy is that you accept what is mundane in your life. You accept your ill health, you accept your problems, you accept your limitations, and because you accept them you freeze them and lock then that energy into a relationship. That is what you do every day. You are a God. You are doing that. Imagine what it would be to get up every morning and defy reality, to start changing what has been normal to you to be supernormal every day. The first day you get up and a few things change but not everything. Is that enough to go back and accept mundane reality, or is it that we are having to create a mind that is so powerful that it can acquiesce the energy field of any lifeform and any situation and change it immediately? What does that take? Constant focus on what is expected rather than what is seen.

When Yeshua ben Joseph was moving his mind up to this lofty state and held it there, he was actually not of this world but indeed, as it has been said, he was in the world. This is the ultimate test, that he had to agree to die as the final initiation. What a final test. How do you defy death? First off, you have to die; otherwise it isn't a test, is it?

Imagine how terrifying that is. None of you are at that place yet but imagine what it would be to fully develop God on this plane. How would he do that? His final test would be to agree to die in front of everyone. So powerful was his mind, which he called "the Father within me," so powerful was he that he allowed the body to die and to go into decay. Then at the appropriate moment he was to reestablish a relationship with the body. Is that possible? Given what scientists say that we do with particles, is that possible? It is indeed.

Where is the loophole here? The loophole is that we are so terrified of life that we never live. We are so terrified of dying that we never live life. No one in this room has the capacity to do that because no one has built up such a wall of reality that "lay the body dead as it is, I will resurrect it." No one has developed that yet because they haven't lived yet. Imagine what kind of body he had then. The body went into physical corruption within three days, and he came back.

Your last lifetime you never went any further than the light. At the light, before you came back to this incarnation, you reviewed your last life. The review took place in your lightbody. It reviewed, unfolded all of the energy, and gave you a living screen to see what you did, who you were, what you accomplished, how you evolved, where you didn't evolve. It just unrolled the energy and allowed it to play. Then once you had decided or made up your mind to come back, you were thinking with a lightbody, not a human body, but you were still cognizant that you could have done better in the physical body. Don't you find it interesting that entities who go to the light talk about viewing their life and that they viewed it with a cognitive judgment? They didn't have a brain. How were they able to make an opinion of what they saw? Because they did have a brain. What was the brain? It wasn't the gray tissue that is sitting up here but it was a brain equal to the body they were inhabiting.

When you die, you move immediately into infrared. It is the psychic realm. From the psychic realm the shaft of light appears and you go down it and you are actually moving from low infrared to the high end of infrared. Then you hit the light. Who is the light? You. It is there that you view everything. While you are making a decision about your physical life, there are four other potential lives or bodies that are enfolded in the light and all you keep doing is agreeing to come back to this one. So you have never changed those four other bodies. They are what we call hidden. We are always recycling the lightbody, the infrared body, and the physical body, but we have yet to use the hidden bodies of the upper four realms.

What does this have to do with Yeshua ben Joseph becoming a Christ? He had to prove that he was accessing the upper kingdom of God, and he had proved it every single way by all of the miracles and the teachings that he imparted. There was one thing that terrified all men in their hearts and that was death. The Hellenistic Jews of that time were the only ones that believed in reincarnation. The Jews of Abraham did not believe in reincarnation. They believed in hell, which was the most terrifying aspect, and that simply meant a shallow grave, that they would be dismembered.

Yeshua ben Joseph had to show to a culture of people

that there was life after death. The way that he had to do that is he had to sacrifice his own life. He had to let the body die and move all the way, unfolding all of those bodies all the way until he is right here and says, "My Father and I are one." He is saying that "My mind is no longer from the House of David in these terrible times. My mind is my Father within me," the first mind. He had to take off every one of those bodies, even the lightbody.[5] He couldn't keep it on. He had to pull off the lightbody, manifest the Blue Body. He had to pull off the Blue Body, which is Shiva, and manifest the golden body. He had to pull off the golden body, go to the rose body, and then he had to go to Infinite Unknown. And only until he did that was he incorruptible.

It was from this state that he resurrected his physical body and gave it life, but what he gave it is eternal life. In other words, his body down here was vibrating nearly at the rate of light. He only kept it slow so that he could interact with people and give them the last teaching. Why was his body radiating so fast? Because that was where his consciousness was. God now was man. He lifted it up and reconstructed its physical matter but he reconstructed it from the point of God, so it was vibrating very fast. When he left, where did he go? He simply raised and kept raising the frequency. In other words, he started a spin around the atom, and then the spin collapsed inward to the inside of the nucleus and it started spinning. All the time he was doing that, all of that spin allowed every one of those particles to go into free space. He was unfolding the seven bodies and when he disappeared, he disappeared at light.

That was only when he was called the Christ, the arisen one. That was the last test. That meant his consciousness had to be one with this so absolutely that not even death could defy that mind. In doing so, we now have great myth and legend and religion circling this entity. What has never

5 See Fig. C in the glossary: *Seven Bodies Enfolded within Each Other.*

been told to you is not that Jesus is going to save your life but rather that he was a master who demonstrated the power of God in man and that if anyone had the eyes to see it, then they would understand. If anyone had the ears to hear the message, they were offered the message. They had to be simple enough to understand the transmutation of the human Spirit into eternity, and it was demonstrated. It wasn't demonstrated just with him. It has been demonstrated throughout the eons in every culture because people soon forget.

What do we have now? We have now a religion around Jesus being the only son of God. That doesn't make any sense because everyone is the sons and daughters of God, not just him, and he can't save you. If he could, he would have done so in the first century. This is his message. How come he didn't teach his disciples this? Because they were simple men. They were fishermen. They were tax collectors. They were people just like you. How could he teach them that? He couldn't. All he could do was to teach them in parables and in deeds.

One fine morning you are going to wake up and realize what I have taught you and you won't sit there struck dumb. You will start laughing and it will come from some wonderful place that you can't stop. You are going to laugh and laugh and laugh because you will see the mirth that lies on the other side of this serious human attitude that everything is oppressive and everything is dreadful. I tell you, the God that I love never judged anyone. It is a giving entity. It is a source. It never says to you, "Well, you want it but you can't have it." It never says to you, "You should do penance before you get it." It never says to you, "Say you are sorry, then I will give it to you."

They should take Yeshua ben Joseph off that cross. What a sad sight. It is to make you feel guilty. I tell you, the God that you are learning about is everlasting life and a life that is so full that you don't even have the mind yet to begin to recognize how much there is yet to experience.

A Life of Virtue

Virtue is a hard road in some senses but it is worth it. Virtue is honesty. Virtue is clarity. It is not using anyone. It is not lying to anyone. It is about being true to yourself. All of your guilt that you have harbored inside, all of the things you have done, all the abuses that you have done to other people are seeds for disease, and ultimately you will be at the hands of your own undoing. The day that we open up and can breathe very clearly is when we forgive our debtors and those who have transgressed against us. When we forgive we allow the past to rest and to no longer occupy those precious moments we have that beg us to renew our life and to become a new person, to reinvent, to give birth to ourself in a way that no one ever allowed us to do before. Forgiving is not reembracing. Forgiving is simply removing them from the aspect of our view that belonged to the past.

Freedom and virtue are the same thing. They come at the cost of the willingness of that which shall enjoy that privilege: the hard work of forgiving your enemies and "letting the dog die," clearing your window, forgiving your transgressors, forgiving the view that you accepted early in your life that led you to such troubled waters, to go all the way to the root of it and to forgive it and to be clean of it, and to entertain no one else in our life that reminds us of the lessness of ourself.

It is a terrible thing when we go looking for trouble. It is a terrible thing when we go dig up our past because ultimately we are the hangman and the hanged. I will be happy, very happy, when all of you learn to reinvent yourself and not to become the lie of the past but who you want to be full-bore, and to love yourself so much that you will never be abused by anyone again and never feel that you deserved it, ever, and to have a quest that says, "I want to know love is a many-splendored thing." I can be an animal but I was born a man, and I was born a woman. I want to know the quality of myself. I want to know that and be able to go after it and live it impeccably and not breed like breeding stock for the sake of the next generation but to bear children out of a union that is that beautiful, that clean, and that pure, to trap no one only to fail to live up to what is expected of you outside of the bed.

So much to learn, and yet it is worth it because you get immortal life. You live long. You have pleasant thoughts and deep ones, and they are not tainted with prejudice. They are not tainted with guilt and shame and ignorance. They are clean, like little children. Christ said only until you become one of these can you enter the kingdom of heaven, and that is nearly the abolishment of the animal to the fairylike existence of pure God, pure youth, pure clarity without prejudice. You are never too old to wake up to be young again, and you are never so bad that you cannot wake up and reinvent yourself and be virtuous.

I have told you a lot of things that if you are really wise, young or old, you would think about and make some choices on. To cherish oneself — cherish it — have you ever thought about cherishing yourself? A unique concept. And love, well, if you are really fortunate and you deserve it, you will find a dancer in your life in the mirror who will dance with you, and you will not know whether it is you looking at a reflection or that you yourself are but one.

Attitude is everything, and you can do this. So be it.
Always yours,

— *Ramtha*

Epilogue by JZ Knight:
How It All Started

*"In other words, his whole point of focus is to come
here and to teach you to be extraordinary."*

5

My name is JZ Knight and I am the rightful owner of this body. Ramtha and I are two different people, two different beings. We have a common reality point and that is usually my body. Though we sort of look the same, we really don't look the same.

All of my life, ever since I was a little person, I have heard voices in my head and I have seen wonderful things that to me in my life were normal. I was fortunate enough to have a mother who was a very psychic human being and never condemned what it was that I was seeing. I had wonderful experiences all my life but the most important experience was that I had this deep and profound love for God and there was a part of me that understood what that was. Later in my life I went to church and I tried to understand God from the viewpoint of religious doctrine and had a lot of difficulty with that because it was sort of in conflict with what I felt and what I knew.

Ramtha has been a part of my life ever since I was born, but I didn't know who he was and I didn't know what he was, only that there was a wonderful force that walked with me, and when I was in trouble — and I had a lot of pain in my life growing up — that I always had extraordinary experiences with this being who would talk to me. I could hear him as clearly as I can hear you if we were to have a conversation. He helped me to understand a lot of things in my life that were beyond the normal scope of what someone would give someone as advice.

It wasn't until 1977 that he appeared to me in my kitchen on a Sunday afternoon as I was making pyramids with my husband. We were dehydrating food because we were into hiking and backpacking. As I put one of these ridiculous things on my head, at the other end of my kitchen this wonderful apparition appeared that was seven feet tall and glittery and beautiful and stark. You just don't expect at 2:30 in the afternoon that this is going to appear in your kitchen. No one is ever prepared for that. So Ramtha at that time really made his appearance known to me.

The first thing I said to him — and I don't know where this came from — was, "You are so beautiful. Who are you?" He has a smile like the sun. He is extraordinarily handsome. He said, "My name is Ramtha the Enlightened One and I have come to help you over the ditch." Being the simple person that I am, my immediate reaction was to look at the floor because I thought maybe something had happened to the floor, or the bomb was being dropped. I didn't know. From that day forward he became a constant in my life. And during the year of 1977 a lot of interesting things happened, to say the least. My two younger children at that time got to meet Ramtha and got to experience some incredible phenomena, as well as my husband.

Later that year, after teaching me and having some difficulty telling me what he was and me understanding, one day he said to me, "I am going to send you a runner that will bring you a set of books, and you read them because then you will know what I am." Those books were called the *Life and Teaching of the Masters of the Far East* (DeVorss & Co. Publishers, 1964). I read them and I began to understand that Ramtha was one of those beings, in a way, and that took me out of the are-you-the-devil-or-are-you-God sort of category that was plaguing me at the time.

After I got to understand him he spent long, long moments walking into my living room, all seven feet of this beautiful being, making himself comfortable on my couch, sitting down and talking to me and teaching me. What I didn't realize at that particular time was he already knew all the things I was going to ask and he already knew how to answer them, but I didn't know that he knew that.

Since 1977 he patiently dealt with me in a manner that allowed me to question not his authenticity but things about myself as God, teaching me, catching me when I would get caught up in dogma or get caught up in limitation, catching me just in time and teaching me and walking me through that. And I always said, "You know, you are so patient. I think it is wonderful that you are so patient." And he would just smile and say that he is 35,000 years old, what else can you do in that period of time? It wasn't until about ten years ago that I realized that he already knew what I was going to ask and that is why he was so patient. But as the grand teacher that he is, he allowed me the opportunity to address these issues in myself. He had the grace to speak to me in a way that was not presumptuous but, as a true teacher, would allow me to come to realizations on my own.

Channeling Ramtha since late 1979 has been an experience. Ram is seven feet tall and he wears two robes that I have always seen him in. Even though they are the same robe, they are really beautiful so you never get tired of seeing them. The inner robe is snow white and goes all the way down to where I presume his feet are, and then he has an overrobe that is beautiful purple. You should understand that I have really looked at the material on these robes and it is not really material; it is sort of like light. And though the light has a transparency to them, there is an understanding that what he is wearing has a reality to it.

Ramtha's face is cinnamon-colored skin, and that is the best way I can describe it. It is not really brown and it is not really white and it is not really red. It is sort of a blending of that. He has very deep black eyes that can look into you, and you know you are being looked into. He has eyebrows that look like wings of a bird that come high on his brow. He has a very square jaw and a beautiful mouth, and when he smiles you know that you are in heaven. He has long, long hands and long fingers that he uses very eloquently to demonstrate his thought.

Imagine then after he taught me to get out of my body by actually pulling me out, throwing me in the tunnel, hitting the wall of light and bouncing back — and realizing my kids were home from school and I just got through doing breakfast dishes — that getting used to missing time on this plane was really difficult. I didn't understand what I was doing and where I was going, so we had a lot of practice sessions. You have to understand that he did this to me at ten o'clock in the morning and when I came back off of the white wall it was 4:30. I had a real problem trying to adjust with the time that was missing here. So we had a long time with Ramtha teaching me how to do that, and it was fun and frolic and absolutely terrifying at moments. You can imagine if he walked up to you, yanked you right out of your body, threw you up to the ceiling and said, "Now what does that view look like?" and then throwing you in a tunnel — and perhaps the best way to describe it is it is a black hole into the next level — and being flung through this tunnel and hitting this white wall and having amnesia.

What he was getting me ready to do was to teach me something that I had already agreed to prior to this incarnation. My destiny in this life was not just to marry and to have children and to do well in life but to overcome the adversity to let what was previously planned happen, and that happening included an extraordinary consciousness, which he is.

Trying to dress my body for Ramtha was a joke. I didn't know what to do. The first time we had a channeling session I wore heels and a skirt. I thought I was going to church. So you can imagine, if you have a little time to study him, how he would appear dressed up in a business suit with heels on, which he never walked in in his life.

It is really difficult to talk to people and have them

understand that I am not him, that we are two separate beings and that when you talk to me in this body, you are talking to me and not him. Sometimes over the past decade or so, that has been a great challenge to me in the public media because people don't understand how it is possible that a human being can be endowed with a divine mind and yet be separate from it.

I wanted you to know that although you see Ramtha out here in my body, it is my body, but he doesn't look anything like this. His appearance in the body doesn't lessen the magnitude of who and what he is. You should also know that when we do talk, when you start asking me about things that he said, I may not have a clue what you are talking about because when I leave my body, I am gone to a whole other time and another place that I don't have cognizant memory of. And however long he spends with you, to me that will be maybe about five minutes or three minutes. And when I come back to my body, this whole time of this whole day has passed and I wasn't a part of it. I didn't hear what he said to you and I don't know what he did out here. When I come back, my body is exhausted. It is hard to get up the stairs sometimes to change my clothes and make myself more presentable for what the day is bringing me, or what is left of the day.

He has shown me a lot of wonderful things that I suppose people who have never gotten to see couldn't even dream of in their wildest dreams. I have seen the twenty-third universe and I have met extraordinary beings and I have seen life come and go. I have watched generations be born and live and pass in a matter of moments. I have been exposed to historical events to help me understand better what it was I needed to know. I have been allowed to walk beside my body in other lifetimes and watch how I was and who I was, and I have been allowed to see the other side of death. These are cherished and privileged opportunities that somewhere in my life I earned the right to have them. To speak of them to other people is, in a way, disenchanting because it is difficult to convey to people who have never been to those places what it is. I try my best as a storyteller to tell them and still fall short of it.

I also know that the reason that he works with his students the way that he does is because Ramtha never wants to overshadow any of you. In other words, his whole point of focus is to come here and to teach you to be extraordinary. He already is. And it is not about him producing phenomena. If he told you he was going to send you runners, you are going to get them big time. It is not about him doing tricks in front of you. That is not what he is. Those are tools of an avatar that is still a guru that needs to be worshiped, and that is not the case with him.

So what will happen is he will teach you and cultivate you and allow you to create the phenomenon, and you will be able to do that. Then one day when you are able to manifest on cue and you are able to leave your body and you are able to love, when it is to the human interest impossible to do that, he will walk right out here in your life because you are ready to share what he is. And what he is is simply what you are going to become. Until then he is diligent, patient, all-knowing, and all-understanding of everything that we need to know in order to learn to be that.

The one thing I can say to you is that if you are interested in his presentation, and you are starting to love him even though you can't see him, that is a good sign because it means that what was important in you was your soul urging you to unfold in this lifetime. And it may be against your neuronet. Your personality can argue with you and debate with you, but that sort of logic is really transparent when the soul urges you onto an experience.

If this is what you want to do, you are going to have to exercise patience and focus and you are going to have to do the work. The work in the beginning is very hard, but if you have the tenacity to stay with it, then one day I can tell you that this teacher is going to turn you inside out. One day you will be able to do all the remarkable things that you have heard the masters in myth and legend have the capacity to do. You will be able to do them because that is the journey. And ultimately that ability is singularly the reality of a God awakening in human form.

Now that is my journey and it has been my journey all of my life. If it wasn't important and if it wasn't what it was, I certainly wouldn't be living in oblivion most of the year for the sake of having a few people come to have a New Age experience. This is far greater than a New Age experience. I should also say that it is far more important than the ability to meditate or the ability to do yoga. It is about changing consciousness all through our lives on every point and to be able to unhinge and unlimit our minds so that we can be all we can be.

You should also know what I have learned is that we can only demonstrate what we are capable of demonstrating. If you would say, well, what is blocking me from doing that, the only block that we have is our inability to surrender, to allow, and to support ourself even in the face of our own neuronet of doubt. If you can support yourself through doubt, then you will make the breakthrough because that is the only block that stands in your way. And one day you are going to do all these things and get to see all the things that I have seen and been allowed to see.

So I just wanted to come out here and show you that I exist, that I love what I do, and that I hope that you are learning from this teacher. And, more importantly, I hope you continue with it.

— *JZ Knight*

RAMTHA'S GLOSSARY

Analogical. Being analogical means living in the Now. It is the creative moment and is outside of time, the past, and the emotions.

Analogical mind. Analogical mind means one mind. It is the result of the alignment of primary consciousness and secondary consciousness, the Observer and the personality. The fourth, fifth, sixth, and seventh seals of the body are opened in this state of mind. The bands spin in opposite directions, like a wheel within a wheel, creating a powerful vortex that allows the thoughts held in the frontal lobe to coagulate and manifest.

Bands, the. The bands are the two sets of seven frequencies that surround the human body and hold it together. Each of the seven frequency layers of each band corresponds to the seven seals of seven levels of consciousness in the human body. The bands are the auric field that allow the processes of binary and analogical mind.

Binary mind. This term means two minds. It is the mind produced by accessing the knowledge of the human personality and the physical body without accessing our deep subconscious mind. Binary mind relies solely on the knowledge, perception, and thought processes of the neocortex and the first three seals. The fourth, fifth, sixth, and seventh seals remain closed in this state of mind.

Blue Body®. It is the body that belongs to the fourth plane of existence, the bridge consciousness, and the ultraviolet frequency band. The Blue Body® is the lord over the lightbody and the physical plane.

Blue Body® Dance. It is a discipline taught by Ramtha in which the students lift their conscious awareness to the consciousness of the fourth plane. This discipline allows the Blue Body® to be accessed and the fourth seal to be opened.

Blue Body® Healing. It is a discipline taught by Ramtha in which the students lift their conscious awareness to the consciousness of the fourth plane and the Blue Body® for the purpose of healing or changing the physical body.

Blue webs. The blue webs represent the basic structure at a subtle level of the physical body. It is the invisible skeletal structure of the physical realm vibrating at the level of ultraviolet frequency.

Body/mind consciousness. Body/mind consciousness is the consciousness that belongs to the physical plane and the human body.

Book of Life. Ramtha refers to the soul as the Book of Life, where the whole journey of involution and evolution of each individual is recorded in the form of wisdom.

C&E® = R. Consciousness and energy create the nature of reality.

C&E®. Abbreviation of Consciousness & Energy^{SM}. This is the service mark of the fundamental discipline of manifestation and the raising of consciousness taught in Ramtha's School of Enlightenment. Through this discipline the students learn to create an analogical state of mind, open up their higher seals, and create reality from the Void. A Beginning C&E® Workshop is the name of the Introductory Workshop for beginning students in which they learn the fundamental concepts and disciplines of Ramtha's teachings. The teachings of the Beginning C&E® Workshop can be found in *Ramtha, A Beginner's Guide to Creating Reality,* third ed. (Yelm: JZK Publishing, a division of JZK, Inc., 2004), and in *Ramtha, Creating Personal Reality,* Tape 380 ed. (Yelm: Ramtha Dialogues, 1998).

Christwalk. The Christwalk is a discipline designed by Ramtha in which the student learns to walk very slowly being acutely aware. In this discipline the students learn to manifest, with each step they take, the mind of a Christ.

Consciousness. Consciousness is the child who was born from the Void's contemplation of itself. It is the essence and fabric of all being. Everything that exists originated in consciousness and manifested outwardly through its handmaiden energy. A stream of consciousness refers to the continuum of the mind of God.

Consciousness and energy. Consciousness and energy are the dynamic force of creation and are inextricably combined. Everything that exists originated in consciousness and manifested through the modulation of its energy impact into mass.

Create Your DaySM. This is the service mark for a technique created by Ramtha for raising consciousness and energy and intentionally creating a constructive plan of experiences and events for the day early in the morning before the start of the day. This technique is exclusively taught at Ramtha's School of Enlightenment.

Disciplines of the Great Work. Ramtha's School of Ancient Wisdom is dedicated to the Great Work. The disciplines of the Great Work practiced in Ramtha's School of Enlightenment are all designed in their entirety by Ramtha. These practices are powerful initiations where the student has the opportunity to apply and experience firsthand the teachings of Ramtha.

Emotional body. The emotional body is the collection of past emotions, attitudes, and electrochemical patterns that make up the brain's neuronet and define the human personality of an individual. Ramtha describes it as the seduction of the unenlightened. It is the reason for cyclical reincarnation.

Emotions. An emotion is the physical, biochemical effect of an experience. Emotions belong to the past, for they are the expression of experiences that are already known and mapped in the neuropathways of the brain.

Energy. Energy is the counterpart of consciousness. All consciousness carries with it a dynamic energy impact, radiation, or natural expression of itself. Likewise, all forms of energy carry with it a consciousness that defines it.

Enlightenment. Enlightenment is the full realization of the human person, the attainment of immortality, and unlimited mind. It is the result of raising the kundalini energy sitting at the base of the spine to the seventh seal that opens the dormant parts of the brain. When the energy penetrates the lower cerebellum and the midbrain, and the subconscious mind is opened, the individual experiences a blinding flash of light called enlightenment.

Evolution. Evolution is the journey back home from the slowest levels of frequency and mass to the highest levels of consciousness and Point Zero.

FieldworkSM. FieldworkSM is one of the fundamental disciplines of Ramtha's School of Enlightenment. The students are taught to create a symbol of something they want to know and experience and draw it on a paper card. These cards are placed with the blank side facing out on the fence rails of a large field. The students blindfold themselves and focus on their symbol, allowing their body to walk freely to find their card through the application of the law of consciousness and energy and analogical mind.

Fifth plane. The fifth plane of existence is the plane of superconsciousness and x-ray frequency. It is also known as the Golden Plane or paradise.

Fifth seal. This seal is the center of our spiritual body that connects us to the fifth plane. It is associated with the thyroid gland and with speaking and living the truth without dualism.

First plane. It refers to the material or physical plane. It is the plane of the image consciousness and Hertzian frequency. It is the slowest and densest form of coagulated consciousness and energy.

First seal. The first seal is associated with the reproductive organs, sexuality, and survival.

First three seals. The first three seals are the seals of sexuality, pain and suffering, and controlling power. These are the seals commonly at play in all of the complexities of the human drama.

Fourth plane. The fourth plane of existence is the realm of the bridge consciousness and ultraviolet frequency. This plane is described as the plane of Shiva, the destroyer of the old and creator of the new. In this plane, energy is not yet split into positive and negative polarity. Any lasting changes or healing of the physical body must be changed first at the level of the fourth plane and the Blue Body®. This plane is also called the Blue Plane, or the plane of Shiva.

Fourth seal. The fourth seal is associated with unconditional love and the thymus gland. When this seal is activated, a hormone is released that maintains the body in perfect health and stops the aging process.

God. Ramtha's teachings are an exposition of the statement, "You are God." Humanity is described as the forgotten Gods, divine beings by nature who have forgotten their heritage and true identity. It is precisely this statement that represents Ramtha's challenging message to our modern age, an age riddled with religious superstition and misconceptions about the divine and the true knowledge of wisdom.

God within. It is the Observer, the great self, the primary consciousness, the Spirit, the God within the human person.

God/man. The full realization of a human being.

God/woman. The full realization of a human being.

Gods. The Gods are technologically advanced beings from other star systems who came to Earth 455,000 years ago. These Gods manipulated the human race genetically, mixing and modifying our DNA with theirs. They are responsible for the evolution of the neocortex and used the human race as a subdued work force. Evidence of these events is recorded in the Sumerian tablets and artifacts. This term is also used to describe the true identity of humanity, the forgotten Gods.

Golden body. It is the body that belongs to the fifth plane, superconsciousness, and x-ray frequency.

Great Work. The Great Work is the practical application of the knowledge of the Schools of Ancient Wisdom. It refers to the disciplines by which the human person becomes enlightened and is transmuted into an immortal, divine being.

Grid^{SM}, The. This is the service mark for a technique created by Ramtha for raising consciousness and energy and intentionally tapping into the Zero Point Energy field and the fabric of reality through a mental visualization. This technique is exclusively taught at Ramtha's School of Enlightenment.

Hierophant. A hierophant is a master teacher who is able to manifest what they teach and initiate their students into such knowledge.

Hyperconsciousness. Hyperconsciousness is the consciousness of the sixth plane and gamma ray frequency.

Infinite Unknown. It is the frequency band of the seventh plane of existence and ultraconsciousness.

Involution. Involution is the journey from Point Zero and the seventh plane to the slowest and densest levels of frequency and mass.

JZ Knight. JZ Knight is the only person appointed by Ramtha to channel him. Ramtha refers to JZ as his beloved daughter. She was Ramaya, the eldest of the children given to Ramtha during his lifetime.

Kundalini. Kundalini energy is the life force of a person that descends from the higher seals to the base of the spine at puberty. It is a large packet of energy reserved for human evolution, commonly pictured as a coiled serpent that sits at the base of the spine. This energy is different from the energy coming out of the first three seals responsible for sexuality, pain and suffering, power, and victimization. It is commonly described as the sleeping serpent or the sleeping dragon. The journey of the kundalini energy to the crown of the head is called the journey of enlightenment. This journey takes place when this serpent wakes up and starts to split and dance around the spine, ionizing the spinal fluid and changing its molecular structure. This action causes the opening of the midbrain and the door to the subconscious mind.

Life force. The life force is the Father/Mother, the Spirit, the breath of life within the person that is the platform from which the person creates its illusions, imagination, and dreams.

Life review. It is the review of the previous incarnation that occurs when the person reaches the third plane after death. The person gets the opportunity to be the Observer, the actor, and the recipient of its own actions. The unresolved issues from that lifetime that emerge at the life or light review set the agenda for the next incarnation.

Light, the. The light refers to the third plane of existence.

Lightbody. It is the same as the radiant body. It is the body that belongs to the third plane of conscious awareness and the visible light frequency band.

List, the. The List is the discipline taught by Ramtha where the student gets to write a list of items they desire to know and experience and then learn to focus on it in an analogical state of consciousness. The List is the map used to design, change, and reprogram the neuronet of the person. It is the tool that helps to bring meaningful and lasting changes in the person and their reality.

Make known the unknown. This phrase expresses the original divine mandate given to the Source consciousness to manifest and bring to conscious awareness all of the infinite potentials of the Void. This statement represents the basic intent that inspires the dynamic process of creation and evolution.

Mind. Mind is the product of streams of consciousness and energy acting on the brain creating thought-forms, holographic segments, or neurosynaptic patterns called memory. The streams of consciousness and energy are what keep the brain alive. They are its power source. A person's ability to think is what gives them a mind.

Mind of God. The mind of God comprises the mind and wisdom of every lifeform that ever lived on any dimension, in any time, or that ever will live on any planet, any star, or region of space.

Mirror consciousness. When Point Zero imitated the act of contemplation of the Void it created a mirror reflection of itself, a point of reference that made the exploration of the Void possible. It is called mirror consciousness or secondary consciousness. See **Self.**

Monkey-mind. Monkey-mind refers to the flickering, swinging mind of the personality.

Mother/Father Principle. It is the source of all life, the Father, the eternal Mother, the Void. In Ramtha's teachings, the Source and God the creator are not the same. God the creator is seen as Point Zero and primary consciousness but not as the Source, or the Void, itself.

Name-field. The name-field is the name of the large field where the discipline of FieldworkSM is practiced.

Neighborhood WalkSM. This is the service mark of a technique created by JZ Knight for raising consciousness and energy and intentionally modifying our neuronets and set patterns of thinking no longer wanted and replacing them with new ones of our choice. This technique is exclusively taught at Ramtha's School of Enlightenment.

Neuronet. The contraction for "neural network," a network of neurons that perform a function together.

Observer. It refers to the Observer responsible for collapsing the particle/wave of quantum mechanics. It represents the great self, the Spirit, primary consciousness, the God within the human person.

Outrageous. Ramtha uses this word in a positive way to express something or someone who is extraordinary and unusual, unrestrained in action, and excessively bold or fierce.

People, places, things, times, and events. These are the main areas of human experience to which the personality is emotionally attached. These areas represent the past of the human person and constitute the content of the emotional body.

Personality, the. See **Emotional body.**

Plane of Bliss. It refers to the plane of rest where souls get to plan their next incarnations after their life reviews. It is also known as heaven and paradise where there is no suffering, no pain, no need or lack, and where every wish is immediately manifested.

Plane of demonstration. The physical plane is also called the plane of demonstration. It is the plane where the person has the opportunity to demonstrate its creative potentiality in mass and witness consciousness in material form in order to expand its emotional understanding.

Point Zero. It refers to the original point of awareness created by the Void through its act of contemplating itself. Point Zero is the original child of the Void, the birth of consciousness.

Primary consciousness. It is the Observer, the great self, the God within the human person.

Ram. Ram is a shorter version of the name Ramtha. Ramtha means the Father.

Ramaya. Ramtha refers to JZ Knight as his beloved daughter. She was Ramaya, the first one to become Ramtha's adopted child during his lifetime. Ramtha found Ramaya abandoned on the steppes of Russia. Many people gave their children to Ramtha during the march as a gesture of love and highest respect; these children were to be raised in the House of the Ram. His children grew to the great number of 133 even though he never had offspring of his own blood.

Ramtha (etymology). The name of Ramtha the Enlightened One, Lord of the Wind, means the Father. It also refers to the Ram who descended from the mountain on what is known as the terrible day of the Ram. "It is about that in all antiquity. And in ancient Egypt, there is an avenue dedicated to the Ram, the great conqueror. And they were wise enough to understand that whoever could walk down the avenue of the Ram could conquer the wind." The word Aram, the name of Noah's grandson, is formed from the Aramaic noun Araa — meaning earth, landmass — and the word Ramtha, meaning high. This Semitic name echoes Ramtha's descent from the high mountain, which began the great march.

Runner. A runner in Ramtha's lifetime was responsible for bringing specific messages or information. A master teacher has the ability to send runners to other people that manifest their words or intent in the form of an experience or an event.

Second plane. It is the plane of existence of social consciousness and the infrared frequency band. It is associated with pain and suffering. This plane is the negative polarity of the third plane of visible light frequency.

Second seal. This seal is the energy center of social consciousness and the infrared frequency band. It is associated with the experience of pain and suffering and is located in the lower abdominal area.

Secondary consciousness. When Point Zero imitated the act of contemplation of the Void it created a mirror reflection of itself, a point of reference that made the exploration of the Void possible. It is called mirror consciousness or secondary consciousness. See **Self.**

Self, the. The self is the true identity of the human person different from the personality. It is the transcendental aspect of the person. It refers to the secondary consciousness, the traveler in a journey of involution and evolution making known the unknown.

Sending-and-receiving. Sending-and-receiving is the name of the discipline taught by Ramtha in which the student learns to access information using the faculties of the midbrain to the exclusion of sensory perception. This discipline develops the student's psychic ability of telepathy and divination.

Seven seals. The seven seals are powerful energy centers that constitute seven levels of consciousness in the human body. The bands are the way in which the physical body is held together according to these seals. In every human being there is energy spiraling out of the first three seals or centers. The energy pulsating out of the first three seals manifests itself respectively as sexuality, pain, or power. When the upper seals are unlocked, a higher level of awareness is activated.

Seventh plane. The seventh plane is the plane of ultraconsciousness and the Infinite Unknown frequency band. This plane is where the journey of involution began. This plane was created by Point Zero when it imitated the act of contemplation of the Void and the mirror or secondary consciousness was created. A plane of existence or dimension of space and time exists between two points of consciousness. All the other planes were created by slowing down the time and frequency band of the seventh plane.

Seventh seal. This seal is associated with the crown of the head, the pituitary gland, and the attainment of enlightenment.

Shiva. The Lord God Shiva represents the Lord of the Blue Plane and the Blue Body®. Shiva is not used in reference to a singular deity from Hinduism. It is rather the representation of a state of consciousness that belongs to the fourth plane, the ultraviolet frequency band, and the opening of the fourth seal. Shiva is neither male nor female. It is an androgynous being, for the energy of the fourth plane has not yet been split into positive and negative polarity. This is an important distinction from the traditional Hindu representation of Shiva as a male deity who has a wife. The tiger skin at its feet, the trident staff, and the sun and the moon at the level of the head represent the mastery of this body over the first three seals of consciousness. The kundalini energy is pictured as fiery energy shooting from the base of the spine through the head. This is another distinction from some Hindu representations of Shiva with the serpent energy coming out at the level of the fifth seal or throat. Another symbolic image of Shiva is the long threads of dark hair and an abundance of pearl necklaces, which represent its richness of experience owned into wisdom. The quiver and bow and arrows are the agent by which Shiva shoots its powerful will and destroys imperfection and creates the new.

Sixth plane. The sixth plane is the realm of hyperconsciousness and the gamma ray frequency band. In this plane the awareness of being one with the whole of life is experienced.

Sixth seal. This seal is associated with the pineal gland and the gamma ray frequency band. The reticular formation that filters and veils the knowingness of the subconscious mind is opened when this seal is activated. The opening of the brain refers to the opening of this seal and the activation of its consciousness and energy.

Social consciousness. It is the consciousness of the second plane and the infrared frequency band. It is also called the image of the human personality and the mind of the first three seals. Social consciousness refers to the collective consciousness of human society. It is the collection of thoughts, assumptions, judgments, prejudices, laws, morality, values, attitudes, ideals, and emotions of the fraternity of the human race.

Soul. Ramtha refers to the soul as the Book of Life, where the whole journey of involution and evolution of the individual is recorded in the form of wisdom.

Subconscious mind. The seat of the subconscious mind is the lower cerebellum or reptilian brain. This part of the brain has its own independent connections to the frontal lobe and the whole of the body and has the power to access the mind of God, the wisdom of the ages.

Superconsciousness. This is the consciousness of the fifth plane and the x-ray frequency band.

Tahumo. Tahumo is the discipline taught by Ramtha in which the student learns the ability to master the effects of the natural environment — cold and heat — on the human body.

Tank field. It is the name of the large field with the labyrinth that is used for the discipline of The Tank®.

Tank®, The. It is the name given to the labyrinth used as part of the disciplines of Ramtha's School of Enlightenment. The students are taught to find the entry to this labyrinth blindfolded and move through it focusing on the Void without touching the walls or using the eyes or the senses. The objective of this discipline is to find, blindfolded, the center of the labyrinth or a room designated and representative of the Void.

Third plane. This is the plane of conscious awareness and the visible light frequency band. It is also known as the light plane and the mental plane. When the energy of the Blue Plane is lowered down to this frequency band, it splits into positive and negative polarity. It is at this point that the soul splits into two, giving origin to the phenomenon of soulmates.

Third seal. This seal is the energy center of conscious awareness and the visible light frequency band. It is associated with control, tyranny, victimization, and power. It is located in the region of the solar plexus.

Thought. Thought is different from consciousness. The brain processes a stream of consciousness, modifying it into segments — holographic pictures — of neurological, electrical, and chemical prints called thoughts. Thoughts are the building blocks of mind.

Torsion Process^{SM}. This is the service mark of a technique created by Ramtha for raising consciousness and energy and intentionally creating a torsion field using the mind. Through this technique the student learns to build a wormhole in space/time, alter reality, and create dimensional phenomena such as invisibility, levitation, bilocation, teleportation, and others. This technique is exclusively taught at Ramtha's School of Enlightenment.

Twilight®. This term is used to describe the discipline taught by Ramtha in which the students learn to put their bodies in a catatonic state similar to deep sleep, yet retaining their conscious awareness.

Twilight® Visualization Process. It is the process used to practice the discipline of the List or other visualization formats.

Ultraconsciousness. It is the consciousness of the seventh plane and the Infinite Unknown frequency band. It is the consciousness of an ascended master.

Unknown God. The Unknown God was the single God of Ramtha's ancestors, the Lemurians. The Unknown God also represents the forgotten divinity and divine origin of the human person.

Upper four seals. The upper four seals are the fourth, fifth, sixth, and seventh seals.

Void, the. The Void is defined as one vast nothing materially, yet all things potentially. *See* **Mother/Father Principle.**

Yellow brain. The yellow brain is Ramtha's name for the neocortex, the house of analytical and emotional thought. The reason why it is called the yellow brain is because the neocortices were colored yellow in the original two-dimensional, caricature-style drawing Ramtha used for his teaching on the function of the brain and its processes. He explained that the different aspects of the brain in this particular drawing are exaggerated and colorfully highlighted for the sake of study and understanding. This specific drawing became the standard tool used in all the subsequent teachings on the brain.

Yeshua ben Joseph. Ramtha refers to Jesus Christ by the name Yeshua ben Joseph, following the Jewish traditions of that time.

Fig. A: The Seven Seals:
Seven Levels of Consciousness in the Human Body

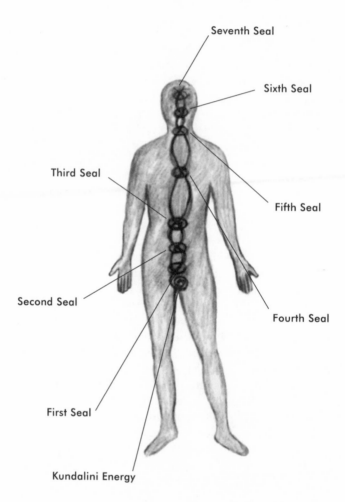

Seventh Seal

Sixth Seal

Third Seal

Fifth Seal

Second Seal

Fourth Seal

First Seal

Kundalini Energy

FIG. B: SEVEN LEVELS OF CONSCIOUSNESS AND ENERGY

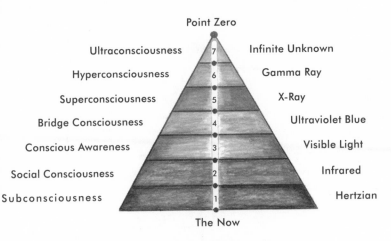

Point Zero

Ultraconsciousness	7	Infinite Unknown
Hyperconsciousness	6	Gamma Ray
Superconsciousness	5	X-Ray
Bridge Consciousness	4	Ultraviolet Blue
Conscious Awareness	3	Visible Light
Social Consciousness	2	Infrared
Subconsciousness	1	Hertzian

The Now

FIG. C: SEVEN BODIES ENFOLDED WITHIN EACH OTHER

Point Zero

7th Level — Infinite Unknown

6th Level — Rose Body

5th Level — Golden Body

4th Level — Blue Body

3rd Level — Lightbody

2nd Level — Infrared Body

1st Level — Physical Body

Fig. D: Consciousness and Energy in the Light Spectrum

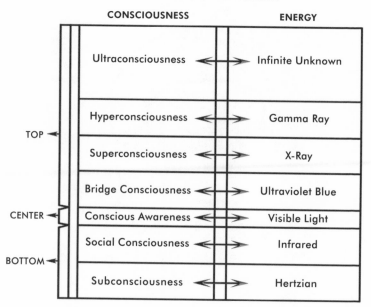

THE LIGHT SPECTRUM

FIG. E: THE BRAIN

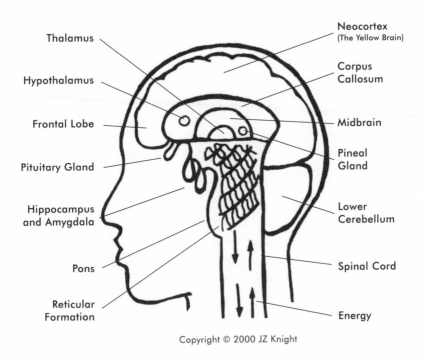

Thalamus

Hypothalamus

Frontal Lobe

Pituitary Gland

Hippocampus
and Amygdala

Pons

Reticular
Formation

Neocortex
(The Yellow Brain)

Corpus
Callosum

Midbrain

Pineal
Gland

Lower
Cerebellum

Spinal Cord

Energy

This is the original two-dimensional caricature-style drawing Ramtha used for his teaching on the function of the brain and its processes. He explained that the different aspects of the brain in this particular drawing are exaggerated and colorfully highlighted for the sake of study and understanding. This specific drawing became the standard tool used in all the subsequent teachings on the brain.

FIG. F: BINARY MIND — LIVING THE IMAGE

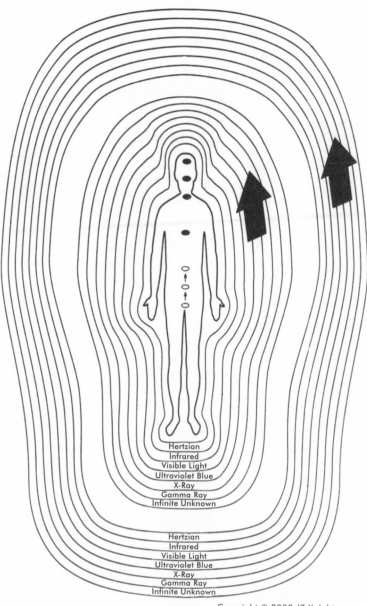

Hertzian
Infrared
Visible Light
Ultraviolet Blue
X-Ray
Gamma Ray
Infinite Unknown

Hertzian
Infrared
Visible Light
Ultraviolet Blue
X-Ray
Gamma Ray
Infinite Unknown

Fig. G: Analogical Mind — Living in the Now

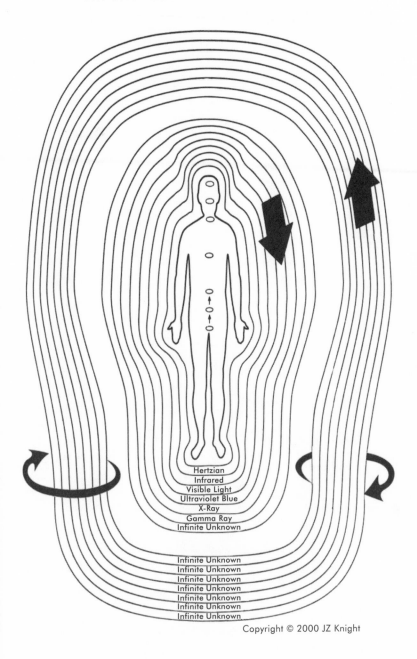

Hertzian
Infrared
Visible Light
Ultraviolet Blue
X-Ray
Gamma Ray
Infinite Unknown

Infinite Unknown
Infinite Unknown
Infinite Unknown
Infinite Unknown
Infinite Unknown
Infinite Unknown
Infinite Unknown

FIG. H: THE OBSERVER EFFECT AND THE NERVE CELL

The Observer is responsible
for collapsing the wave function of probability
into particle reality.

Particle   Energy wave   The Observer

The act of observation
makes the nerve cells fire and produces thought.

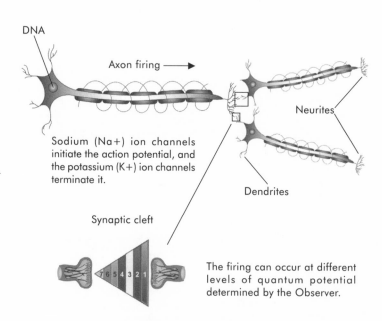

DNA

Axon firing →

Neurites

Sodium (Na+) ion channels
initiate the action potential, and
the potassium (K+) ion channels
terminate it.

Dendrites

Synaptic cleft

7 6 5 4 3 2 1

The firing can occur at different
levels of quantum potential
determined by the Observer.

Fig. 1: Cellular Biology and the Thought Connection

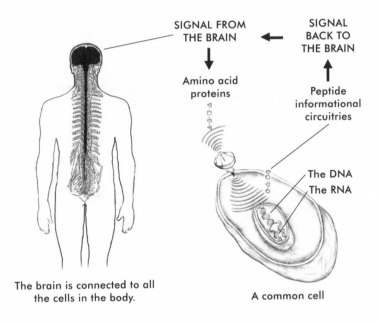

SIGNAL FROM THE BRAIN

SIGNAL BACK TO THE BRAIN

Amino acid proteins

Peptide informational circuitries

The DNA
The RNA

The brain is connected to all the cells in the body.

A common cell

Fig. J: Weblike Skeletal Structure of Mass

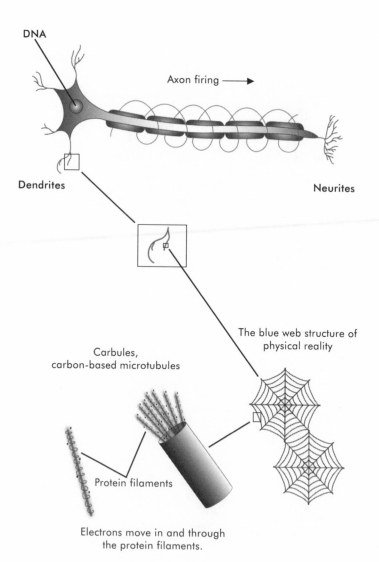

DNA

Axon firing ⟶

Dendrites

Neurites

The blue web structure of physical reality

Carbules,
carbon-based microtubules

Protein filaments

Electrons move in and through
the protein filaments.

FIG. K: THE BLUE BODY®

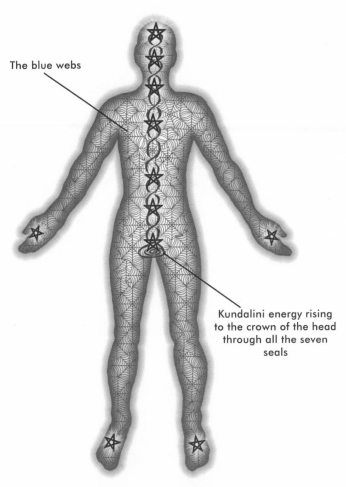

The blue webs

Kundalini energy rising
to the crown of the head
through all the seven
seals

Ramtha's School of Enlightenment
THE SCHOOL OF ANCIENT WISDOM

A Division of JZK, Inc.
P.O. Box 1210
Yelm, Washington 98597
360.458.5201
800.347.0439
www.ramtha.com
www.jzkpublishing.com